SUBURB'N NDN

SUBURB'N NDN

Nymeria Publishing, LLC

First published in the United States of America by
Nymeria Publishing LLC, 2022

Copyright © 2022 by Hidden Bear

All rights reserved. Except as permitted under the U.S. Copyright Act of 1976, no part of this publication may be reproduced, distributed, or transmitted in any form or by any means, or stored in a database or retrieval system, without the prior written permission of the publisher.

Nymeria Publishing
PO Box 85981
Lexington, SC 29073

Visit our website at www.nymeriapublishing.com

ISBN 979-8-9851572-5-3

Printed in U.S.A

To my beautiful Bride; Together or not at all.

And to my Uncle Rod, thank you for being the elder and teacher I so desperately needed.

Introduction

Suburb'n ndn

Noun. An Indigenous person who grew up "off reservation," mainly amongst non-Natives; or An indigenous person who has fully assimilated into the colonial culture but maintains tribal affiliation; or A native person who was not raised traditionally and lives in an urban area.

My indigenous experience is rarely represented in the media. I am Mechoopda, but a few generations ago my ancestors decided the best path forward was assimilation. Adopt the culture and religion of the European nation that had invaded their home. Growing up I didn't learn any history or culture of the Mechoopda people. I was told as an enrolled tribal member we occasionally received money, but we weren't really "Native." I grew up learning American history from an assimilated mindset. And I grew in knowledge of the bible, its languages, rituals, and Christian American culture. My parents unaware of this ancestry worked diligently to raise me to be the best version of myself. An effort for which I am deeply grateful. (Hey Mom and Dad, I love you, and look I wrote a book.) The previous generations had simply stopped passing it down. Assimilation had done its job in my family line and eradicated our native identity. In 2016, everything changed for me. The Standing Rock Sioux tribe mounted a peaceful resistance to the construction of the Dakota Access Pipeline. I watched the footage of water protectors being sprayed with water cannons and pepper sprayed in the face. They did this to children and elders. I was horrified. But I was also inspired as I listened to the elders speak. And I was absorbed by the chants of "Mni Wiconi" or water is life. Something deep within my spirit awakened.

    I called my Uncle Rod who had been a part of the tribal administration and in his professional life works with tribes and nations across the country. I asked him if he could teach me anything about the Mechoopda culture. Over the years he has become my elder and my teacher. Our stories, our tribe's history, our family history, our cultural practices were taught to me and I even made my own ceremonial dance regalia. As I learned I felt this deep, profound revolution in my soul. I found a place of belonging and identity among my ancestors. I was transformed.

    I grew my hair out from the buzz cut combover I had worn for much of my life. After years of patience, I swelled with pride at the sight of my traditionally braided hair. It was such a sacred moment I was blessed to share with my beloved wife. The rush of an internal identity being displayed so proudly and publically. However, as I embraced my indigeneity, invalidation always found a way back into my life. "You look like Jesus," was the most common statement I've heard. Or when I explained growing my hair out as a cultural practice people would ask, "Like Khal Drogo?" A character from the Television Show Game of Thrones. A fictional man of a fictional people from a fictional place. These helped me see a reality previously absent in my life. Indigenous people are supposed to be in the past. People never want to hear about current indigenous issues just the "cool" stories of resistance to genocide or ancient cultural secrets they can feel special for knowing. But always just the stories of the past; of a rich culture targeted for extinction.

Cultural genocide has been an effective tool. For example, the most common question I receive is "How native are you?" Referencing blood quantum levels. This question is meant to destroy my identity. If I am not pure-blooded enough then they don't have to listen to me as an indigenous voice. This question and others like it made me feel small when I was younger and I wanted to hide this part of myself. When I was a kid growing up I stopped telling people I was Mechoopda. Occasionally, I still feel I have to prove myself native enough.

I was talking with my Uncle and I expressed these feelings to him. He told me he had felt the same way before, then comforted me. Simply saying: "You belong to the tribe." I am Mechoopda because the tribe claims me. It's a simple and objective truth but it was powerful. This has given me the bravery to own who I am in full. Descendant of both colonizer and the colonized. And in this acceptance, I recognize my responsibility to my people. To learn to be fully Mechoopda and pass this knowledge to the next generation. And to honor and share my journey from fully assimilated to fully de-colonized. This book is a memorial of my journey and the full acceptance of my Suburb'n Ndn Identity.

You will notice this book is broken into three sections. Each section covers an aspect of my decolonization starting with Land. I had grown up with the colonizers' philosophy toward land. Land is a tool for extracting resources. It might be extracting oil, coal, or timber. Or generating revenue streams like rental fees, profits from businesses, or profits from farming. Indigenous people see land as a living being to honor. This understanding is the main reason so many tribes and nations engage in conservation efforts. The largest protectors of biodiversity are indigenous peoples throughout the world. The more I was exposed to these ideas I felt my views change. Land isn't just a resource but a birthright passed down to the next generation. A birthright intercepted by colonization. I cannot walk the sacred mountains of my people without paying for a private tour. The Sutter buttes in central California are surrounded by private property and you need permission to access them. The stones my ancestors used to cultivate their foods and medicines are still there. The wild carrots they once consumed still grow on those mountains. I cannot participate in their lifestyle. I have not just lost a "resource" I have lost my place of belonging. In this section I wrote about my love for the California lands of my people and the beauty of the natural world. Of how I have rediscovered my birthright in new ways and in new lands.

    The next section is about my tribe. The relationship between the European colonists and indigenous nations is filled with horrors and learning the past was difficult. Realizing its impact on the present was a revelation. As I wrote about my people my attention turned from past, to present, and ultimately to the future. What will being Mechoopda mean as my children step into adulthood. I filled this section with dedications to those who preceded me and their sacrifices. I also wrote about my experience as I am the present dream they once fought desperately to preserve. And now it's my job to ensure my children can live in complete confidence in their Mechoopda identity and wear it proudly. I cannot steer the fate of my people or the nation I live in but I will use my words to honor all generations. And hopefully imagine a harmonious indigenous future.

Finally, the last section is about me. I have struggled to reconcile the colonized identity with my indigenous one. I often felt there were two parts of me at war with each other. Finding a way to integrate two parts of myself took years of journaling, prayer, poems, and reflection. I have found peace at last. The deconstruction of my personhood was painful and long. Anyone who has been through a similar process can tell you this is difficult work. But on the other side is a complete and confident person. I am grateful for the struggle. It gave me the confidence I have today to be my full self. The once hidden indigenous part of me is free and in the light. I hope sharing this personal part of my journey inspires you. I hope this book guides you to free the hidden parts of yourself.

To unhide the bear.

Land

Homeland

West Coast

Coastal cliff lines

Pacific waves and beach signs

Wetsuits, hoodies and sunglasses

Cold sands and salty eyelashes

Saltwater taffy and In-N-Out

Seals and grey whale spouts

McClintock's portions and fresh artichoke

Ollaberry pie and hot spring soaks

Graffiti tunnels to downtown Sacramento

San Diego filled with navy boats

Take BART to in-city trolley ways

Birthplace in my heart remains

East Coast

Summertime fireflies

Humidity hike and tan lines

Wolfpack driving through cookout

Triple Threat and drive thru shouts

Tar heel, stain on my boots

Tobacco plants and oak roots

Blue Ridge Mountain overlook

Fall colors pose for breakfast nooks

Neuse river flows clear waters

Pine trees and dogwood flowers

Beasley's Chicken and honey

Marshlands and river gully

Birthplace of my descendants

Southern home contentment's

Flights between magnificent beauty

Each place calling melodious to me

In all places I stand

Call them my homeland.

Home

Concrete driveway and Bradford pears
Creaking steps and yearning porch
Sheltered chairs to watch leaves amber in fall
Gazing as the pear trees bloom in late February

My land of organized grass lanes
Pre-ordained trees and poorly kept bushes
Roof patches and an old fence
Big backyard for my children

The house moans as I pass through it
Telling stories of the previous tenants
New door handles but on old stove
Cooking fry bread in a cast iron skillet

Back porch with old, chipped paint
Weeds on the side and out of control vines
An old shed housing my tools
Cedar smells released to delight

Splitting wood with my axe

The songbirds pass the time with tune

Fire pit filled with ash from nights of memories

A/C system sings to match the hummingbirds

The suburbs smell sage around it

Nature respected in its place

Everything as I ordain it

Blessed by the creator

This land is mine.

Central Valley

I-5 aimed south

Through a rolling dustbowl

Brown grasses fill my horizon

The wildflowers have since wilted

Dried out land cracking

Fence line rows like tombstones

Billboards promising future fruit

Green yielding solely from sprinkler

The coastline mountains

Weave through hillsides of decay

Withered and arid winds

Through tunnel the coastline delivered

Fog teasing the moisture

The highway perched on granite crags

The surfers abide in the waves

Beauty beside decay

Hotel room smells of salt
Redwood giants in the entryway
Cold mornings and warm coffee
Wetsuits and waves

Salt water taffy dances
Clam chowder warms me
My thought returns to desolation
But the boardwalk returns joy

Heading north again
The coastline waves goodbye
I see storm clouds on the horizon
Thundering and flashes of light

Striking the ground in the valley
Sparks find ordination on dry fields
Ash is left behind as witness
Flames hunger endless

Red hues fill my windows

Ash storms over the city

Glowing coals my bed

Lethal air and rancid smell

Beauty in a painful burn

To new lands I turn

Estom Jamani

Rising peak presides over the valley

Surveying life from the beginning

Start and end to my journey

The Bear hibernates, grinning

Birthplace of humanity

Descending from the middle mountain

Harmony with life founded in balance

The Bear rises for accounting

Acorns dotting the hillside

Centuries old holes in the rock

Ground down for life to continue

The Bear breathes from the mountain top

Surrounded by cultivated land

Profit over the sacred space

People cut off access

The Bear weeps rivers from its face

Long extinct the Bear rests

Mountains remains through time

Bear's death releases its soul

Spirit finds the mountain's spine

Resting one last time on middle mountain

It's rock pressing onward

Crying out for one last breath

The Bear's roar echoed by song birds

Heliophilia

It again encircles glowing increments

Splashing purple and red hues

Skies canvas blush

Sacred routine returns renewed

Flowers rejoice in song

Birds blooming their wings

Trees sing through their leaves

A dawning hope it brings

Rest ending upon re-energy

Ocean lawding praise

Swirling coastal grass wave hello

Delicacy for my ancient gaze

Nyctophilia

The ocean turns its back

Dark purples splash the sands

Starlight asserting its control

Full moon emblazoned over man

The owls call loud but wings are silent

Crickets play orchestras to the dark

Peer through veil and behold

Each placing their nocturnal mark

Paced rhythms of silence

A backdrop of constellations

Laying in long grass, eyes wide

Masterpiece, all my relations

Winter Flowers

Ice sways as it falls

With clouds over head protecting it

It lands on the ground

Covered by its siblings and swallowed

Yet this one finds a new path

Gently resting on a suitor

The red bloom's petals flash like fire

Delicate the petal holds up the Ice

More Ice seeks out the beauty

Soon the bloom is covered in Ice

Though consumed its beauty shines through

Undeterred by its guests

The flowers color violent

Fighting back despair in winters depths

Existing in defiance of the cold

Beauty through the Ice

Feeding home from its stamen

Petals adorn the green leaves

Stitching together an Ice mosaic

A raw, unrefined, stained-glass window

Birds fly overhead and witness

Drawing all attention to its glow

The winter flower thrives

A winter vigil for hope

Birthplace

Nosebleed tickets to an A's game
Chanting for each player's name
Rocking the gold and green blanket
Hot dog and chips my banquet

King's game with no elbow room
Purple and black t-shirt cannon zoom
Webber, Peja and Bibby scoring
Arco Arena decibels soaring

Raider Nation chanting loud
Camera swooping over crowds
The black hole represents my team
Believing against losing streaks

Loving my home and cities
2001 hopes crushed completely
Playoff runs ended but I'm still proud
My cities Oakland and Sac Town

Greenfield

Take the exit off the highway

Pull into town past the Rite Aid

Memories walking there

Outside in the fresh air

Roll down main street

Houses and shops to see

Vineyards and farmland backdrop

Mexican restaurants and suburban plots

Pull into the tiny church parking

Grandfather's organ howling

Across the street a billboard on an empty space

My grandparents' house still in place

Greenfield "Welcome" sign just up the road

Said goodbye for the last time unknown

Ripon

It's a blue house on a side street

With a hallway radiator for heat

A drawer in the kitchen corner has chocolate donuts

A kid's table and one for the grownups

Enchiladas in the oven smell fills the room

I get a full belly just from its fumes

Card games cause shouting and kids with presents

A thousand clocks chime at an hour's presence

Attic explorations and tee times with the men

Hot chocolate in the golf cart keeping score with a pen

One day I found donuts for the last time

I grasped the attic railing for a final climb

I didn't know it would change so fast

I just want those hidden donuts back

Condor

I see them soaring across the sky

Broad wings splayed out circling in flight

Strange heads, black feathers curved beaks

Characterized as evil; death on sight

But I find them to be beautiful

Those black feathers a cape of tenebrous flight

Their patience unmatched as they soar

Landing gently, head bowed in afternoon light

Their unseen beauty lies in what they seek

The dead bodies laying about the landscapes

Spying them out from the terrible heights

Amidst the wild and city finding the shapes

Those things left for dead and forgotten

Cast to the side by common apathy

The most reviled, the end destination

And yet they seek it out voraciously

A witness to notice the dis-noticed
Seeking out the last resting places
Find the death and decay of the planet
Peering into finality their bare faces

And rather than turn its eye away
It stays remaining with the dead
On the roadside or trail finding this despair
Devouring the void, keeping it well fed

Witness the beauty of this creature
Turning decay into sustenance and new life
Recycling what was forgotten and left to rot
Into a beautiful bird swooping through daylight

The death of a thousand ancient stars
Was never consumed by the dark
But the scattered decay was renewed
As blood in my veins and the sun's spark

My life brought forth from entropy

There is beauty in everything lost.

But at my end I hope the Condor sees me

As I pay life's final cost.

Sacred City

Crowded streets make my feet dance

Bouncing on heels, pausing and taking a step

I hear the drum beats in the cars as they pass

The singing from honking horns and police sirens

Every stranger participating in the dance

Swirling in patterns as they travel their journey

The morning fog hanging in the air like sage smoke

The warmth from the pavement mimicking fire

Creator honored in the city on sidewalks

From the earth the city rose, how could it not be sacred?

Apartments building like villages

Community care programs for the elderly

Speaking different accents in different cities

The same language but we still must listen

Artistry flourishing underground and in alleyways

The city vibrant in indigenous ways but blind to them

People have lost the love of wild places

Between each other, their mother, and our relatives

The city rose from the earth but lowered its people

We have become lost with the sacred

But like the city it can be rebuilt

The land healthy and the city thriving

If our spirits would reach to each other

Let our cities listen to the indigenous sounds it produces

And return our spirits to heal

Native Lunch Break

Clock out, take off my work ID

And cross the street

Pavement carved into forest

Surrounded by the ancient cityscape

A narrow path through towers of pine and oak

Precursor to downtown alleyways

Branches like awnings shade me

The wind agitates the treetops

Singing the songs of old growth traffic

Eardrums cracked by crows and hawks

Emergency sirens of invaded territory

Spider web scaffolding makes perilous my walk

The edges of the pavement groomed

Nature for separation not interlock

Moss covers the outermost edge

Roots surfacing under the pavement

Smooth surface turns to mossy mountain ranges

New growth expands nature's reclaimant

My soul dangles from branches

Spanish moss mosaic identity

Steps timed to un-played drum beats

Will the wild stay with me?

Cross the street

Clock In, Take out my work ID

Trees

Plant them they provide shade

Or fruit

Chop them down they provide warm shelter

Sap can be syrup or glue

Leaves create stunning beauty

They hold you up

Height to draw our gaze upward

Broad trunks for hide and seek

Nesting branches for new life

Flowers spark awe and joy

Year after year providing and giving

Destroyed for us to read new knowledge

Our minds like branches seeking sunlight

Trees never move or go to war

Split them they will simply grow back

Wearing scars and pain plainly

Complimenting destruction with delicate petals

Reaching toward the heavens

Bend them they simply seek the light

Growth never ceasing

May we ever follow in their path

Hyperion

Stand aloft the cliff over the edge of beauty
Driftwood, boulders and seagulls infill
The crashing swells overwhelm me
I survey the forest behind in awe

The fog resting high in tree top spires
Clutching tightly sage and eagle feather
I enter weaving steps between vegetation
Ferns tickle my ankles as I am swallowed

The ravine filled bark feels delicate in my hand
Solid and giant the tree defies my eyes gaze
Unable to penetrate the forest protector
Clouds of the forest and leaves hidden among them

I search for my prize, Hyperion
A whisper tickles my ear; guiding
I reach a sacred place and hear him
"Kneel." Hands trembling again
To the side an Elk stands presiding

A Condor lands silent and venerating

Hyperion mocks the sky with its reach

I dig near the base and lay to rest my feather

Burning a white sage leaf I pray

That I might find peace at Hyperion's root

Salmon

Leaping through pathways upstream

Amidst treachery to nest

Home resounding through rapids

Tides playing counter melody

Shimmering scales flashing in air

Writhing bodies ever onward press

Predators encircles hungry

Open claw and jaw distended

Numbers abound through leaping runs

Awash in dawnlight hues

Chinook life in turbulent streams

Dwindling life in progeny

Preservation rewilding the rivers

Resurgence

Let the salmon run; free.

Vineyard

Vineyard lacing across hilltops
Latticework of fruit delicacy
Harvesters churn out perfection
Beautiful wine in perpetuity

Aquifers and irrigation lines carved
Neat lines of food system artistry
Trucks of bountiful supply streak
Fresh fermented wine commodities

Summer grasses brown in eyeline
Fresh vineyards sprinkler mist
The water trapped and rationed
Supplies making jealous fish

The vineyard supplying life
Overwhelming fruitful choices
The water limited and flowing
Amid the driest voices

Can we not live in balance?

Vineyards and wildflowers both

Is life not worth more than commerce?

For the earth I have spoke

Urban

From the ground they rose

Made of metal and stone

Perches only birds dreamed of

Glass reflecting the sun

Smooth walkways fell from the sky

Complimenting the architect's eye

The Earth always the supplier

As we erected each tower

Striping the landscape in stone ways

Evolving beyond each previous phase

We grew up in the arms of our mother

Built cities, towns and homes with cellars

She gave up her best gifts to us

And how do we repay that trust?

What do we return to empty mine shafts?

What is planted alongside the train tracks?

What is returned to ocean farm ways?

What extra is grown to replace?

What do we owe this home of ours?

Everything! and yet we yearn for Mars?

One more place filled with resources?

Have we considered our choices?

In order to build there must be cost

Without our Mother Earth we are lost

Cities have left us cut off to her, unknown

What do we owe the one that gave us home?

Empty

The machines come first

Automated saws and giant claws

Trees fall in seconds

Broken branches and trunk detachments

A trail of broken stumps

Brush crumpled and machines rumble

The land resting again

Birds homeless and squirrels treeless

Bulldozers take their aim

Pushing roots and expelling soot

Grinding away the remnants

Wildlife fleeing and nature seceding

Level dirt resting in this place

Uneven dirt and construction work

Beams of steel reaching to the sky

Plumbing laid and foundation paved

The building placed in a matter of months

Area surrounding is prepared for pounding

Flattened and the black top pours

Smooth tar for parking cars

A few squares left unpaved

A sapling planted

The business failed after three months

The Sapling grows and the lot is fallow

The space is now unused and rotting

Nothing is left the whole space bereft

Empty

Ground

Tectonic plates drift

Rivers make pathways

Glaciers graze across

Tread down by beasts

Ploughed and sliced

Cities heavy weight crushing

Blasted and mined

Oil extracted

Gold ripped from place

Uranium bored out

Our feet rarely leave and always return

How can you own what you burn?

People

Show me

Can you show me the way?
Stone ground acorns shells
Mati and stories tell

Can you show me the way?
Artwork basket weaving
Hunting unceasingly

Can you show me the way?
Elderberry clapper sticks
Drum beats and dancing hips

Can you show me the way?
White sage before me
Ceremony performing

Can you show me the way?
Ancient practices revived
The Kumeh alive

Can you show me the way?

Responsible for the land and creatures

Economic restoration and the tribes futures

Can you show me the way?

Casino plans and tobacco sales

Mortgage loans and powwow tales

Can you show me the way?

Regalia made and re-made

Language learning how to say

Can you show me the way?

Grass games again played

Young ingenious reclaim

Can you show me the way?

Urban native belong to the city

Matching my oxfords to my Skili

Can you show me the way?

Back to the middle mountain

Back to where my people were founded

Echo

The Bear roars from Sutter

Restoration in echo

One people listen and dance back

Termination

Land held in trust

Culture to dust

Treaty in rust

Land no longer in trust

The land owned and taxed

Promises broken relapsed

Deception breaking backs

Hegemony levied immoral Tax

Dissolve the people

Bow to the steeple

Freedom a steep hill

Guarded by congresspeople

Taxing reparations

Backing termination

Desecration of nations

Unimproved station

Lies for easy ownership

Broken treaty relationship

Policy of forced fit

To disband tribalship

The era ended in name

But it's still the same

Standing rock proclaims

Land Back to native names!

Diaspora

1967 Termination the verdict

Landless indigenous people

Land owned but never improved

Taxed out by a 1000 needles

Run off the original land

No sacred place or reserve

Language and traditions fade

Generations miss history preserve

Spread out among the immigrants

Left to their own devices

Pain, wandering, assimilation required

Indigenous culture in crisis

Wandering the urban landscapes

Wondering if we would ever return

Exile filling our eons future

For our land we yearn

Return

1992 landmark verdict

Recognized by colonial eyes

Established council and land

Hope on horizons skies

Traditions uncovered and taught

Konkow apps and colonial recognition

Taking our place in Butte County

All under mechoopda re-acquisition

Home at last return from exile

Mechoopda relation over percentile

Reclaim

To return

Turning back time

Placing things in proper place

Ordered from destruction

Souls torn from their homelands

Culture ripped from their hands

Stripped of all they once called familiar

Cast into exile without heritage mirrors

Told "forget everything that can't be sold"

Ancient practices cheapened takes its toll

Our people mining their spirits just to eat

Sold at retail prices on colonized streets

Powwows forming a monolith out of unique peoples

Forcing fake props into American steeples

Once again, the people rise to reclaim

Remember our spirits and ancestors' names

Rising to return our identity as a nation

Rebuilding from colonized desecration

Reclaiming our culture as sacred

Not sold but held in exultation

Reviving the indigenous person to awake

Traditional or urban we reclaim our rightful place

Extinct

"Having no living member"

All living specimens lost

Laid to rest in granite tombs

The grizzled bear's exhaust

The salmon swim fearless

No claws to elude

Extinction by hunter

No tombstone hewed

Victim of the hunter

Of Termination era

Rancheria dissolved in treaty

Promises by Chimera

Court cases rage against us

Our tribe discounted as less

Ten years of extinction narrative

Economic rights long oppressed

But ere the bear rises

"Having no living member"

This does not define us

For the people remember

The grizzled bear is in history

But our tribe is still here

Holding place on our land

Facing weapons of fear

The salmon shutters at our roar

Claws sharpened anew on rock

The bear shattering granite

Power aw in our aftershock

Roundhouse

The drums echo through dusk
Smoke billows from the center
Sounds of song fill me
Burning sage my nostrils enter

Dancers in a flurry, capes of feather
Whistles blast to the rhythm
Feet shuffle and move with brilliance
Ancient ritual a gift once given

Practices given us by the Oankoitupeh
Heritage passed to each generation
Kumeh unbroken for centuries
Roundhouse in hardship and celebration

Broken down and burned in assimilation
Lost the art, and silent fell the songs
The drums were stored and decayed
Past a hundred years since those wrongs

Yea, look upon our restoration

Roundhouse is rebuilt anew

Ancient songs rediscovered

Capes and clapper sticks are still few

The ancestors reaching out to new generations

Kneeling in humility I answer back

I begin my work to reclaim

With struggle I walk reclamation path

Hope

The middle mountain consecration

Reformed for restoration

Land once again under our protection

Wildlands for animal conservation

Pride of place restored

A new future's floor

Generations battled on

To restore our song

Mechoopda flag wavers

Fresh air savors

Poker chips and tobacco leaves

Blessing like redwood trees

Newsletters and administrators

Councils and curators

Urban natives reclaim

Overturn the ancient pain

Not lost to histories pages

But earning due wages

Stewards of our rightful land

Even without deed in hand

Our calling echoed in our ears

Mechoopda for a thousand years

Regalia

Pull the string tight on the spacing board
Weave the shuttle right and tie it well
Feel the cordage in your hands
Weaving; feeling what the ancestors felt

This cape draped around you
Dancing; feeling the creator speak
Singing a song to the one who made you
Each item made is a decolonized feat

Laying each feather in its place
Reconstructing the old ways with new hands
Weaving together history with the present
Ancient vision and flicker feather bands

Cleaning out eagle bones and burning sage
Honoring the dead through ceremony
Making each element for the dance
Wearing shell necklaces of abalone

Learning the stories from our elders
Teaching language classes to the youth
Reading our histories once again
Seeking out our ancestors roots

Make it by your own hand
Build your own spaces for storage
That each piece is honored well
Tying together your own cordage

Let the regalia speak of your name
Fingerprints across every surface
That you may bless the creator
Creating as you prepare service

Collect each item on your own
Inherit it from family if you must
Let your traditions ensure time
These cannot be held in trust

Hold sacred each skill you learn

Making nets, beading, and securing feathers

Each one is resistance

Reclaiming our ways through teaching each other

Be patient and treat each phase as blessing

Taking time to honor the past

Be mindful of the present as you create

For the future turns to the present too fast

Let your artwork be medicine

Reviving the elders and youth alike

To rebuild and heal their souls

Regalia is warrior dress for the fight

MMIW

Red Hand Prints

Weeping sons and stolen sisters

Vanished like spoken whispers

Trafficked to unknown

And Red Hand Prints

Police reports filed under apathy

Old photographs living memory

Lost souls in bereavement

And Red Hand Prints

New reports devoid of revelation

Police system avoided reformation

Congress legislates in apathy

And Red Hand Prints

Children without mothers

Isolation smothers

Nations still languish

And Red Hand Prints

Red stains the sands

Death at cold hands

No witness found

And Red Hand Prints

Swarms of lethal locusts arrive

Indigenous woman stolen lives

Action seldom taken

Red Hand Prints

For the Murdered and Missing

For the lives of indigenous

Red Hand Prints

River Cut

Carrying 500 year burdens

Generations groan agony

White River Rapids cascade

Leaving no traditional identity

The River flash flooding

Gaslighting history books

Economic tampering policy

Money makes the river crook

The fight leaves many bloody

Tear gas, prison cells at AIM

Kidnapping leaders for defending

Telling us we're actually the same

The River rages greater on the horizon

Hands quivering to reach out

Futility to keep on this way

What if I take a different route

The sweet peace of oblivion

No longer paddling through rapids

Drifting through six feet lagoons

Death was always going to happen

Why fight against night

Dusk comes without our control

The river destroying in greed

What could be my role?

Then I think further still

My family and nation need me

How will we rise again?

Is there a vision to be free?

Dam the River!

Like the beavers teach us still

Dam the River!

Lie bloodied on protest hills

Dam the River!

The black snakes come to poison

Dam the River!

War chants noise at sit-ins

A fist held high screaming

"You can't take my life!"

Choosing the war instead

The river split by the knife

The banks may overflow

Though war surround you

Truly you are worthy

Colonization yours to subdue

Do not let the River drown your mind

Instead cling tightly, mighty warrior

Against darkness and invasion

We rage and erect barrier

The future requires your participation

Without you lost we are as a nation

Stones From the river

They wanted drops of golden sunlight

Coming from every direction

Seeking to harvest

The stones from the river

And they called us "digger"

We sought out food from roots

While they blasted mountains for stones

They thought less of the peaceful people

Trading gems for cotton garments

Seeking to harvest

The Stones from the River

Captured our lands and marched

Lead us away like cattle

Destroying our language

Ending the sacred ceremony

Seeking shelter on Rancheria

As they extracted

Seeking to harvest

The Stones from the River

Hunting the bear to extinction

Blasting holes into the earth

Panning riverbanks to soot

Seeking to Harvest

The Stones from the River

Over a hundred years later

Nothing has changed

Still desiring resources

Seeking to Harvest

The black snakes from the forest

Poisoning the waters

Rivers they once sought after

Never satisfied and always

Seeking to Harvest

Items of different names but always

The Stones from the River

Blue Print

My compass is cracked

Clouds hiding the stars

No GPS in my pocket

No gas left in the car

Before me are two roads

One goes left and the other right

Both bare my footprints

Each proclaim against me indict

The left replays memories

Who I have been for years

Assimilated, apathetic, uninvolved

Filling my eyes with tears

The right paints fears

Rejection from the "real" people

Cries of unbelonging

Turns my resolve feeble

Neither path can be tread

They both bare thousands of my footprints

In front of me are miles of untamed wilderness

My identity has no correct blueprint

Follower

Endless names in endless loops

Reframed, reformatted, recycled

Monuments of marble and stone

Filled to the brim with revival

Theology cooked with seasoning

Taken in unbridled gluttony

Steeples abundant on the turtle's back

Herding in the wealthy guilt

Forgiveness preached to power

As bombed buildings wilt

Songs of admiration for liberty

Invisible pain by drone delivery

Creator can you not see?

Is salvation meant for me?

From

Wilderness my home

City life is all I have seen

Where do I come from?

Where will I rest?

Destinesia

Wilderness I have created
Picture frames of the past hover
Pathways and unfurled choices
Who am I now?

Walls of myself to dust
Destruction by new perspective
Soul left in disquietude
Who am I now?

The definitions thrust upon me fade
The shadows no longer my home
At once I arrive at ipseity
Who am I now?

Frames taunt with incomplete reflections
Labels providing clarity
Clarity providing chains
Who am I now?

The feather in flight

The bible hovers

Fighting each other in battle

Who am I now?

Arrived to build myself

Materials abound but tools scarce

I gasped hold the frames

They break in my hands

Hovering slices merge mosaic

Who am I now?

Crawfish

I went walking in the rain

Followed a worn path through the trees

Saw something strange ahead

A crawfish walking slowly among leaves

The pale sky and brown patchy earth

Left nothing but sadness to experience

But in contrast was this pink

Small crustacean walking mysterious

Why was it here in the forest?

There isn't a lake or river nearby?

As I walked past I was confused

Then later on my walk it was clarified

I'm a crawfish lost in the woods

Finally a truth I could really rest in

When I returned to that place the crawfish had left

Whether to its destination or its death?

I still do not know.

Unanswered

Can my heart reside in two chests?

Can I love two lands?

Two people?

Can one man have two souls?

The Conversation

Oh you're native American, but like how much?

Why are you asking that?
To erode my connection to the past
I'm native despite blood quantum delineations
As if colonizers decide who is first nation
My tribe enrolled me in my place
My ancestors created me a space

Didn't you get like free education?

No I didn't. Boarding schools cost us everything
Kidnapping, colonizing, culture killing rings
Illegal religions and nuns with abusing hands
All in the name of "kill the Indian save the man"
Suppressing who we are so they could take our land
Pretending to be heroes offering helping hands

But you didn't grow up traditional or on a reservation?

You're right colonization does work

From Roundhouse dancers to desk clerks

Just 3 generations for assimilation

Outlawed cultures and outlawed nation

The land wasn't needed or critical

Full of resources and seen as available

Warfare, disease and surviving 1.5

That's the percent of indigenous still alive

Descendant from the original tribes

Our remnant carry on, survive

Economic tampering on reservations

Leading to further oppressed nations

And yet we are still here

Reclaiming traditions from incorrect history books

Building regalia for my first dancing look

I can count to three in my tribe's lost language

Tribal members preserving so it wouldn't languish

I didn't grow up traditional I was colonized

But slowly I see with renewed indigenous eyes.

Well, no offense but you just look white. How can you claim it?

Yeah maybe I don't look like my ancestors

But I made my *Sikli* by hand choosing each feather

My spirit connects to the land and my people

My soul cries to towering trees not towering steeples

I carry their spirit with me as I pray to creator

Skin color doesn't reveal my native nature

But you don't have an Indian sounding name?

Again colonization strips our culture

However, I see my red soul as granite sculpture

It beckons me to a new name

One just for me to show I'm not the same

Call me Hidden Bear as my namesake

As among my ancestors' place; I take

What do I call you?

Indian

Native American

American Indian

Indigenous

Tribal member

Primitive

Redman

Merciless Savage

Digger

Redskin

Full Blooded

Half Breed

One-quarter

One-Eighth

One-sixteenth

One-Thirty Second

White

American

Assimilated

You can call me Hidden Bear.

Skin

Skin is a mirror reflecting feelings

When I survey my own reflection

My vision is muddled with madness

In the mirror three tones splash my canvas

Each coloring in a different version

In sunlight delivers my conversion

The sun revealing the invisible ink of my ancestors

Imprinted on my DNA; bleeding through colonization

Resting atop my arms; inheritance within me.

Prayers written on two tones of the same arm

Umber hues reflecting my ancestors' embers

The pallid underside reflecting antiquity

Self-enmity poured onto the surface

Skin revealing two worlds pigment and privilege

Cloaked in the color of colonization

Bleached out by the sun of assimilation

I cannot carve out different parts of me like bloodied fractions

I can't point to the ancient blood running through my actions

I'm not two halves at war

I am one Mechoopda

Box

If you walk into my house on the floor

You will see a wooden box inside the door

Made of pine and a lid that's not secure

Lined with Cedar to protect its stores

For some it's called a medicine box

I just call it my blessed spot

What's inside that sacred item

Is it secret? Why do I hide them?

That is where I keep my soul

City living carves into my heart a hole

Only my traditions fill that empty space

So depression, alcohol, pain don't take that place

Finding my identity at the end of the day

The box is there to replay

All of the decolonizing I have done

Remind me that I am my tribe's son

I am descendant of the people of the garden

And the box reminds me what to put my heart in

Mixed

Turquoise rings and Apple Watches

iPhone Zoom meetings and eagle feathers

Proof of enrollment letters and faxes

Burnt sage, prayers for cultural tethers

Pumping gas and black top

Hawk screams and fry bread

Calling tribal office for rent assistance

Weaving regalia for my head

Playing out business man

Writing poems on computer screens

Protecting nature on my land

Seeking what urban native means

Can I learn traditions and survive?

Does city living crush my spirit?

Can indigenous mean this life?

If Creator calls warriors will I hear it?

Blending two liquids as one

Mixing as oil and water

I'm confused by my place

Can I wear regalia and white collars?

Acceptance

Glance in the mirror

Straighten my tie, check my hair

Pulled back tight

Walk into the reception taking care

"I have an appointment with the manager"

My voice cracks with nerves

They smile, "Have a seat they will be with you"

Seeking bravery reserves

Run to the bathroom for another check

Did any hair slip out of the hair tie?

Should I have just worn it down?

Should I explain or try to justify?

The pain of culture clashing

What if they don't take me seriously?

I really need this job

Just interact gregariously

Don't explain your culture for a job

You shouldn't have to do that

No one looks down at long hair anymore

Remember dignity always intact

Leave the bathroom and clutch my resume

Scrolling through powwow pictures

"Right this way." I follow

Praying, passed artificial light fixtures

Glass beads

Stringing around my neck

Smooth dangling beads

White, pristine and hewn

Ancient and brand new

May I wear them well

Spirit

He wandered the earth looking for me

Traveling the coastal forests near the sea

Climbing through canyons and mountains

Through waterfalls, rivers, and geyser cannons

At middle mountain I missed my appointment

He left in search of his lost anointed

Cast out into the wild places

Without him I would not be safest

So, he sought me out across the land

From oceans swells to desert sands

When he finally found me no longer young

Nonetheless he gifted me a native tongue

Giving me at last my indigenous voice

Raising my tribal flag my spirit rejoice

Writing the journey of my spirit into verse

To find myself I had traveled the universe

Decades long in search of where I had wandered

Return to myself, my spirit is now honored.

Seek

I read the old stories

I take in the pictures

I hear the old language

I listen for elder whispers

I research for their names

I follow the family tree

I pray to the Creator

I visualize the village and me

I dream of the roundhouse

I hear the clapper sticks

I smell the sage swirling

I dance in the Kum's midst

I weave together regalia

I secure each item in place

I prepare my spirit for connection

I dance seeking creator's face

I feel the one who made me

I hear them call my name

I listen to wisdom descend

I am heard by the same

I no longer seek a missing piece

I have found my spirit again

I no longer worry

I note my thoughts with pen

I hear ancestors clamor praise

I know it's because I am found

I have longed for this day

I have citizenship on our sacred ground

I descend from those who suffered

I inherited a resilient soul

I belong to the first nation

I may at last find home

I hear the celebration

I feel their identity become mine

I welcome their songs

I will show the world our shine

Scarring

I have them on my body

One from an accident trying to sell knives

One from a surgery trying to save my life

Three from a bike accident in college

No helmet led to a face bandage

I have them on my heart

From too many places called home

Relationships maintained by telephone

Having it broken and healed on repeat

Life's failures, disappointments, and grief

I have them on my soul

From colonized heritage lost

To death's overbearing cost

Feeling alone against the anguish

Fluent in pain's cursed language

I have scarring across every part of me

And all together they display my beauty

The end

In the end

What did I answer?

The call?

The question?

The purpose?

In the end

What did I find?

A history?

A people?

A land?

In the end….

What did I define?

A belonging?

A word?

A place?

In the end

I am me

In the end

Does that give me peace?

Found

I have found my location in time
Identity concretes my spine

Lasting truth resonates my soul
At last, reconstruction, I am whole

Through fire of doubt and pain
I have found myself still sane

Eyes fixed on blurring starlight
Guiding focus in tight

My name Hidden Bear
Alternate names remains there

I no longer see through opaque eyes
Modern imagery with ancient ties

Regalia clad indigenous man
Suit and tie businessman

Two feet, two shoes, two souls

One man, one heart in folds

A tapestry of stories weaved

From mental cells I am freed

I need not let go of any part

Rather embrace fully my heart

I kneel in awe of my transformations

Through time and pain a new foundation

I have come alive once more

Hidden Bear. Hear Me Roar!

Acknowledgments

I would like to acknowledge the people of the Tuscarora Nation and Lumbee Tribe. On whose ancestral homelands I live and wrote this book.

Hidden Bear is a poet and a member of the Mechoopda Indian Tribe of Chico Rancheria. He currently resides in Durham, NC with his wife and children. And he loves Peanut Butter M&Ms.

www.ingramcontent.com/pod-product-compliance
Ingram Content Group UK Ltd.
Pitfield, Milton Keynes, MK11 3LW, UK
UKHW042002230426
12048UKWH00009B/505